Within The Darkness

Dedicated to a fantastic Website, VampireRave.com

By Lisa Hiatt

Karmina's Song

Though thou body lay to rest,
Still thine love beats within mine chest.
Death is but another plane,
Earthly binds restrain.
Though angel wings unfurled,
Mine love securely burrowed.
I bide mine time till we're together once more,
To walk hand in hand along heaven's shore.

By Lisa Hiatt

Scarlet

The vein courses scented rose,
Pricked by thorn the color flows.
A scarlet, fluid intensely deep,
So soft but tender in slumber sleep.
Obscure beauty in death undead,
A damning state to rest the head.
Petals fall like scarlet rain,
Plucked from roses in vain.
The body a vassal like scarlet rose,
In nature's womb grows.
So fragile is the life thread of all,
Carelessly cut do fall.
Soulless demon dares to drink,
Render all who venture extinct.

By Lisa Hiatt

Beloved

O decayed lover, Thanatos slave,
Embedded winter's kiss in thy grave,
Thou whisper from cyanosis lips,
Caressing with frigid fingertips.
Mine heart frozen with tempered ice,
Bereaved by life's sacrifice.
Cradled in the bosom of death domain,
Hades stole thee from this earthly plane.
Mine barren arms grieve,
But mine ardor eternally cleave.
The shades extend their greedy jowls,
Thou dragged to Hades bawls.
I descend to search evermore,
Pursuing thee to death's shore.
I know not the hour of mine demise,
Our rejoining brooks no compromise.
For not even Hades can staunch love,
Mine lover, mine beloved.

By Lisa Hiatt

Scarlet Jewels

Scarlet jewels laborious drain,
Exposed from jugular vein.
Sabering sharply deep,
Slashes rendering sleep.
Crimson eyes watch the scene,
Collecting the bounty's stream.
Oh what demon horde,
Swiftly stabbing fanged sword.
Thief of ebbing life,
Selfishly taking the sacrifice.
Wintery heart no compassion shown,
Horded treasure all his own.

By Lisa Hiatt

IT

It lies in 7x3 box,
While eternity tick tocks,
Slumbering insomniac sleep.

Biding its time,
Its thirst sublime,
Keeping scarlet eye on sheep.

Evilly smiling with sharp fang,
Shushing the hunger pang,
Just a box full of half rotted bone.

Void of darkness its soul,
Crawlies its company in the black hole,
Cold in its grave with worn tombstone.

Reading passerby,
"Watch your step!" Wonder why?
Until it drags you to its lair.

Unsacred ground musky, barren,
Humans but mutton-carrion,
Whoever said life was fair.

By Lisa Hiatt

Ever-after

Obscure beauty ebony rose,
Black and deep as it grows.
Bathed in moonlight bliss,
Thriving on a glowing kiss.
Evil comes to destroy its splendor,
Petals fall gently tender.
Rain weeps in the satin night,
Laundering blackened evil white.
Ivory rose hope eternally springs,
Evil comes with vengeful stings.
Darkness comes with evil laughter,
But pure Love promises ever-after.

By Lisa Hiatt

Pearl

Celestial pearl in satin sky,
Solitary basking on high.
Keeper of love,
Companion of stars above.
Wishes sworn on the glows,
Fragrant memories midnight rose.
Inhale the scented night,
Wishes granted on starlight.
Lovers keep your eyes above,
The moon is sending you love.

By Lisa Hiatt

Winter

Solemnly easing new tide,
Lovers embrace to the chill outside.
The crystal rain falls deep and white,
Cloaking the ground caressing the night.
Patterned glass fogs the windowpane,
The tinkle of ice, sunlight wane,
Winter kiss's the cherry cheeks.
Earth silently sleeps.
The wind howls a triumphant gale,
The icy hand cold and pale.
Butterfly chrysalis sweet slumber,
Till spring awakens with wonder.

By Lisa Hiatt

Frozen

In stasis yearning frozen sleep,
Neglected damning eternal keep.
Icicles form in the air,
Above the screams of despair.
Hold me, rock me, comfort my pain,
Stop the voices make me sane.
Colder and colder feel the hunger,
Help me it's dragging me under.
The scarlet rose incased in ice,
Enthralled in strangling vice.
Entwined in love keeper of night,
Lover, hold me forever tight.

By Lisa Hiatt

Wolf Bane

Midnight falls dark and dreary,
Senses open full and weary.
Harvest moon so divine.
All this malevolence alone is mine.
Amber eyes watchful sight,
Glowing with full-moon lit night.
Shattered silence midnight howl,
Demon dredged from hell's bawl.
The taste of crimson so sweet,
Disemboweled at my feet.
Glorious freedom from God's rule,
Worshiped darkness deviously cruel.

By Lisa Hiatt

Celtic Whispers

Emerald eyes my Bonne lass,
Beloved of times past.
Celtic whispers Bonne's name,
War the culprit to blame.
Unfair winds blowing sorrow,
Promises of a better 'morrow.
Buried on namesake's Hill,
The flowers immaculate still.
Daisy yellow the dress she wore,
Beloved of times before.
When love was fair my Bonne lass,
With passion held within my grasp.
Patience my Bonne I thee follow,
Promises kept on the wings of 'morrow.

By Lisa Hiatt

Fallen Princess

Fair thee well I bid thee,
Perched in window Ivory.
Flaxen hair, spun with gold,
Keeper of mine heart thee hold.
Cometh conquering hero knight,
Rescue mine fallen princess plight.
Scaling Ivory high tower,
Climbing n'er neither weak nor dour.
But mine fallen princess bids me,
To scale the tower of Ivory.
Cometh I with heart in hand,
For cometh I to take mine stand.
To look mine lover in the eye,
Evermore climbing towards heaven's sky.

By Lisa Hiatt

Wolfing Hour

Howling for celestial mistress,
Yearning for a midnight tryst.
Harvest moon smiles in vain,
Demon morphing feels the pain.
Amber reflection in his eyes,
Glowing fiery unhallowed arise.
Claws reach for her love,
Alas shallow beauty from above.
Mournful echo moonlit shine,
Lost forever till end of time.

By Lisa Hiatt

Zombie Love

The smell of death,
Upon the breath.
Carrion such an addictive taste,
Tissue and sinew nothing to waste.
Biting through,
To get to you.
Come let me inside,
Open wide.
Sweet meats,
Tongue, intestine, cheeks.
Your heart don't deprive,
I want to eat you alive.

By Lisa Hiatt

Concrete Angel

Whimsical sentinel so stoic,
Ashen stone staunchly heroic.
Still darkness illuminating moon glow,
If only you can tell us what you know.
Wisdom in the depths of granite eyes,
Ever watchful towards heaven's skies.
Locked in stasis, standing alone,
Surrounded by marble tombstone.
Vertiginous smile on stone lips,
Cold and smooth to fingertips.
Wings weathered extend,
Anticipating heaven's wrath to descend.
Frigid beauty in winter's chill,
Sentry of cemetery hill.

By Lisa Hiatt

Cheater

O cheater of death,
Thou thief of breath.
Chaste kiss cyanosis crimson lips,
Frigid chill the taste drips.
Like sand it runs through fingers,
The metallic taste lingers.
Sharp teeth glisten,
Mine tempoed heart, listen.
Fear but a heart-beat away,
The trepidation thou will stay.
Immortal love a promise n'er sorrow,
Kept forever till 'morrow.
Slumber now my lover,
Eternity we discover.
Winter's bed awaits in unhallowed ground,
Slowly thou heart's beat finds no sound.
Sadly thee I bid Adieu,
Soon thou re-awaken anew.

By Lisa Hiatt

Willow

I weep for thee,
Under the willow tree.
Where grass embraces you lover,
While cloud sullen gray cover.
Your eyes once robin's egg blue,
Destiny took my lover true.
Come bury me,
Under the willow tree.
Next to my beloved fair,
My heart heavy has no more life to spare.
The river beckons me,
To follow thee.
The angels turn away,
As I bow to pray.
Please take my mourning plight,
Carry me to his light.
So bury me,
Under the willow tree.
Saying good-night to the moon,
I follow thee soon.

By Lisa Hiatt

Voices

What are the voices in my head?
So dark and dreary the things said.
Fallen angels at my feet,
Whispering of obscure deceit.
Tangled in ivy vines,
A prisoner held with poison binds.
Voices whispering in my ear,
Telling me things I hate to hear.
Out damn spots my hands so stained,
Panic enclosed like I'm chained.
Drenched in sweat I want to shout,
Washed hands but won't come out.
Endlessly running down narrow paths,
Escape just out of my grasp.
Urgent whispers calling me back,
The way from hell pitch black.
Caress me my lover in the night,
You make everything alright.
The echoes still haunt my waking hour,
Lover you have the healing power.
Make love to me with reverence I pray,
Only you chase the voices away.

By Lisa Hiatt

Apocalypse

Winds whisper of apocalypse,
Drying words upon parched lips.
Dying world the sea of drought,
Nature screams murderer out.
What man will take a stand?
Yester-year slips hourglass sand.
The air weeps oil stains,
Seeping chemicals in our brains.
Eyes wide open, closed with stupidity,
So death of all mores the pity.
Cracker Jack schemes,
Last minutes dreams.
The day dawns undead,
History unread.
Caring hearts broken,
Good deeds unspoken.
Lost platitudes,
Nonchalant attitudes.
Children fend for yourself,
Line-up to the food shelf.
Empty boxes line the stalls,
Stomach's rumbling hungry calls.
Barren trees,
Fall to your knees.
Death Angel wings unfurled,
Beg forgiveness to an uncaring world.

By Lisa Hiatt

Dark

Falling into darkness, the black abyss,
Constantly yearning for your dark kiss.
Promises of eternal wonder,
You quench the hunger.
Passion burns bright red,
Into the darkness I bled.
Eyes glowing with unholy desire,
Drowning in the fire.
You call my name,
I'm drawn to your flame.
Catch me as I fall,
For you I grant all.
Forever seeking your embrace,
My dark angel fallen from grace.
Even hell can't hold my lover,
Together forever we'll discover.

By Lisa Hiatt

Jealousy

Emerald nectars coat,
Choking my throat.
Lips drip saccharine sweet,
Heart at your feet.
You gaze in wonder,
As you fill the hunger.
The way your eyes drink,
Without a blink.
She oozes by,
I stifle a cry.
Her come hither sashay,
Eyes all look her way.
Envious consuming,
Lost in the fuming.
Why doesn't he eye me that way?
Beseeching hurry away.
Laboriously she walks by,
Kicking sand in the eye.
Throwing towel in surrender,
All gorge on her splendor.

By Lisa Hiatt

Sandman

Woven in dreams from slumber-land,
Fantasy world epic wasteland.
Story fragments spun in cerebellum,
Sandman's conundrum.
Impatiently awaiting sleep-time hour,
To impose a gritty shower.
Insomniac pace furrowed floor,
Alarm clock screeching Nevermore.
Warm milk glides down,
Impolite rumbling sound.
Sandman inflicted plight,
Never a sleepy-night.
Working nights must stay awake,
Wishing so for a vacation break.
Darkness sounds the witching hour,
Bedtime sheep bow to his power.
Eyes grow heavy with sand,
Chasing woolen peeps in slumber-land.

By Lisa Hiatt

Quickening

Quietly you creep; you creep to my door,
Silently I weep, I weep ever-more.
The tales you spin, you spin so smooth,
It glides down like gin and vermouth.
Coughing, choking stealing my breath,
Wanting, yearning a quickening death.
Quietly you steal, you steal the years,
Silently I accept, I accept my fears.
The tales you tell are of living life,
Twisting, turning death's dull little knife.
So wrinkles and gray hair follow your wake,
While slowly I die with each breath I take.

By Lisa Hiatt

Homeless

Cold winter chill seeps to the bone,
A soul lost no place to call home.
Possessions packed in a squeaky cart,
Bitterness for the homeless heart.
Fingertips bitten from frosty morn,
Dirty clothes raggedly torn.
Paper stuffed in baptized shoes,
A quick fix from all the sad news.
Curious looks, squeaking on by,
No tears from a stranger's eye.
Shelters full to the brink,
Thirsting for that last drink.
The eyes of the young fill the hall,
Santa won't make his curtain call.
Toys are wasted when you ain't a tree,
Christmas dinner chef ala Boyardee.
Judgment is seen from others it seems
Shattering the last of illusive dreams
Christmas all wrapped with pristine bow,
Rattling change in a cup to show.
So Santa is dressed all in festive red,
While contemplating next to rest the head.
The turkey awaits the carving knife,
Some livin' the homeless life.

By Lisa Hiatt

Fallen Rose

Amber is she this fallen rose,
Kissed by harvest moon glows,
Her rapturous face lifts to drink,
Shooting star's twilight blink.
Tears fall from velvet skies,
Her satin petals baptized.
Romancing the starry sky,
She beckons random butterfly.
Embracing the sweet aromatic night,
She mourns absence of sunlight.
Pluck not this fallen rose,
For she's fickle where she grows
Her thorns deeply lancing,
Warm winds lead her dancing.
Fallen rose thriving in moonshine,
Her story told once upon a time.

By Lisa Hiatt

Death

Disguised as disease,
Taking life in degrees.
You live to inflict pain,
Driving holes into the brain.
Your eyes ebony black,
Emotional turmoil a midnight snack.
You keep an angelic smile on your face,
To beckon others to a dark place.
Your eyes a mirror to a bottomless soul,
Welcoming others to the hell hole.
A premise that you truly care,
But in reality you're a nightmare.
Death is a name,
You solemnly claim.
An equal opportunity employer,
A first class destroyer.
It's not a matter of how, but when,
All living will find the end.

Lisa Hiatt

Darkwood

I beckon thee to Darkwood,
Where many heroes once stood.
To conquer evil nearby,
Where fowl refuse to fly.
The sounds of silence shatter,
All peace of mind no matter.
An evil presence fills the head,
The still air dead.
Turning back is no option now,
For it has crept up on you somehow.
So turning to see,
What has crept upon thee?
The mind so easy to trick,
Death not so quick.
Imagination mine best tool,
For thou are the fool.
Heroic quest ignored,
Mind's eye envisions Satan's horde.
Running deeper to escape,
The unavoidable mind rape.
Exhaustion sets in,
Hopelessly lost wondering.
Darkwood night,
Never awakens to sunlight.
Icy fingers chill to the bone,
Winds eerily whisper. "Welcome home."

By Lisa Hiatt

Grand-daddy's Demise

Oh I hate to tell ya how granddaddy died,
It brings such a tear to my eye.
I remember that Christmas day,
When granddaddy got blown away.
See granny wasn't the best of cooks,
Tryin' new things got her strange looks.
Granddaddy never said a word,
Even when she burnt the Christmas bird.
Learnin' after 50 years,
To accept the good with the jeers.
He ate her cookin' without a peep,
And mostly passed gas in his sleep.
Sometimes silent sometimes loud,
Granddaddy was always so proud.
Never wantin' to seek medical attention,
It was just too private to mention.
So that Christmas she served baked beans,
The gas was the worst you've ever seen.
Granddaddy didn't feel so well,
And with the second helpin' he began to swell.
Didn't help that granddaddy had hemorrhoids
So flatulence wasn't something he enjoyed.
It started about half past eight,
The smell too bad to contemplate.
Rollin' in agony clenching his rump,
His rear end getting rather plump.
Awakenin' granny with a bang,
One final groan of agonizing pain.
A little after midnight,
He just gave up the fight.
It is said that the coffin walk,
You'd swear that granddaddy let out a squawk.
And each time the Hurst hit a bump,
A loud protest came from his rump.
It stated plain to see on his casket,
That granddaddy blew a gasket.
And on his tombstone it read,
Here lies granddaddy farted himself dead.

By Lisa Hiatt

Amber Gold

Amber gold falling down,
Dry as a peanut brittle sound,
Crunching under feet.

The wind like a cantankerous mule,
Braying like a fool,
Snowflakes icy sweet.

Falling into autumn a hurried pace,
Smiles on an orange pumpkin-ed face,
Collectors at your door in spooky attire.

Cats arch with sharp teeth,
Awaiting the Christmas wreath,
Burnt leaves in a roaring fire.

Settling for graham crackers and a chocolate kiss,
Warmed with hot cocoa bliss,
Smells of marshmallow steam.

Hibernating till spring,
Robin's cheerily sing,
Awaking to a thawing dream.

By Lisa Hiatt

Snow Angels

Tongues catch icy crystal designs,
Frosting on evergreen pines.
Icing air exhaling steam,
Christmas card Hallmark dream.
Mittens, hats, snow suits,
Toes toasty warm in boots.
Heralding silent night,
World glitters diamond white.
Cozy prone on creamy ground,
Closed eyes, listening, silent sound.
Caught under hypnotic spells,
Making Noel snow angels.

Lisa Hiatt

MIA~ Cheeky Elf

This is a horror story in the first degree,
Missing in action, what a mystery.
Santa had many helpers he called them elves,
They helped keep toys on the shelves.
For all the good kids all over the land,
Santa was very thankful for the helping hand.
Now one elf if I can recall,
Was cheekiest of them all.
Liked to sit in Santa's choice chair,
He'd state, "Well it's comfy there."
The story goes that Christmas day that glistened,
This certain elf had just gone a missin'.
His hat and belled shoes lay in Santa's chair,
No one expected them to just be laying there.
They sent out the basset hound,
To see if he could be found.
But sadly not finding a trace of him,
Losing hope as the twilight grew dim.
Others swore they could still hear his voice,
When Santa sat in his chair of choice.
Santa being rather stout,
Couldn't figure out.
Why his Santa suit,
Kept calling him a brute.
Gasping elves point and stare,
Santa wondered why they pointed there.
Finally in the mirror he looked back,
Found the missing elf in his butt crack.

By Lisa Hiatt

Mine King

Dreamless in slumber sleep,
Sentinel of mine keep.
Vigilant to thou mighty roar,
Thou breath sings a melodious snore.
Hard at labor throughout the day,
Boosting of dragons slay.
In a corner stands tarnished armor aged,
Awaits new wars waged.
Monies come few but far between,
And still in thou eyes I be queen.
Our palace be but thatch and stone,
It still shines a place called home.
Walls crumble with disrepair,
But within love resides there.
So sleep in sweet slumber mine king,
'Morrow unknown what it may bring.
But know like the tides of time,
In mine heart thou love rests divine.

By Lisa Hiatt

The child

Her death came as no surprise,
The cancer brooked no compromise.
Warring emotions, relieved she suffers no more,
But missing the friend you adore.
You know life will end,
But still you mourn for a dear friend.
The nurse enters to remove tubes wired,
Unconcerned just another one who expired.
Barely looking your way,
Unaware you died too that day.
Tears burn down a cheek,
No answers to the questions you seek.
She covers her peaceful face,
The walls close-in this space.
She exits the door left open,
The heart shattered broken.
A child passes and looks in,
Comes close, touching skin.
A sweet smile on angelic lips,
Contrasting cool fingertips.
"It's alright to cry."
His voice like a gentle sigh.
"But know she's not far,
This soul is now a bright star.
Did you know that we possess,
Within our very chest.
The star's holy light?
And though she had to give up the fight,
Her soul shines in the night.
To guide others to heaven's door,
Enlightening heaven's floor."
Turning to go,
Head all aglow.
Watching him walk away,
His little wings sway.

By Lisa Hiatt

Lullabye

Hush mine child hush,
Thou cross cheeks ablush.
Know thou art secure,
Innocence kept pure.
Rock mine child rock,
Heed twilight hour on clock.
Muffled cry in the night,
Eyes so aglowing bright.
Rest mine child rest,
Be assured thou be blessed.
Dwell in draped slumber-land,
Dusted by the sandman.
Lips sing sweetly,
Melodious so greet thee.
Eyes so drowsily slip,
Hitching breath on soft lip.
I be sorely amiss,
To deny a tender kiss.
Upon downy haired brow,
I promise a vow.
Mine arms thee hold,
Until I be old.
Someday soon I be abed,
And thou must rock me instead.

By Lisa Hiatt

Parsley, Sage, Rosemary, and Thyme

Foliaged embracing arms,
Canopy's willowy charms.
On Sage river lethargic sleep,
Obscure rapids running deep.
A gentling lullaby trickles by
Echoing Wolf's mournful cry
Pillow plump clouds race,
Neither worried about the pace.
Midsummer's eve Thyme air,
Dandelion crown adorn hair.
Contented sigh on Rosemary lips
Trailing Parsley watered fingertips.
Tenderly rocking afloat,
Warbling cricket's off-keyed note.
Fireflies synchronized harmony,
Sleepy chuckles for their revelry.
Star speckled heavens, moon hung low,
Basking harvest sphere aglow.
Ginger reflected moonbeams,
Fragrances whisper sweet dreams.

By Lisa Hiatt

A Soldier's Noel

The skies were ablaze that Christmas night,
Bombs and gunfire lit darkness light.
From out of the darkness on an angel wing,
A sweet melody began to sing.
A baritone voice soon rang out crystal clear,
Even the enemies couldn't help but hear.
One by one the gunfire silenced as he sang,
And not one bomb decided to rain.
The brave valiant soldiers wiped a tear,
Listening to the sweet voice so crystal clear.
All looked to the other to see who sang,
But the darkness covered the voice that rang.
Emotion clogged all to humble silence,
For a moment forgotten was all the violence.
Until the last note of Silent Night,
No one wanted to finish the fight.
A miracle happened, suspended in time,
All was peaceful and divine.
Then in the sky a bright star did adorn,
A reminder to all, Christ was born.

By Lisa Hiatt

I Forgive

On my honor I solemnly vow,
That I'll forget what you did somehow.
Daddy, you tried your damnedest to keep me down,
By beating my little body into the ground.
By taking my innocence from me,
How could I have called you daddy?
When I wiped my tears of blood,
You'd slap me back in the mud.
You tried to break me with words so cruel,
By calling me stupid and a simple fool.
By hitting me till tears finally dried,
Till something swelled inside.
I came to despise,
All the hate in your eyes.
A gold lesson I learned,
A parent's respect is earned.
After everything said and done,
I know I'm the stronger one.
Because daddy, I still live,
You've taught me I can forgive.

By Lisa Hiatt

Bonne Queen

High on Kingdom's emerald hill,
Next to crystal waters ever still.
Mother Nature, Bonne queen,
Crown of dandelion and leafy green.
Where crickets trumpet her wake,
Sits she so sad in her heartbreak.
Season, her colorful king,
Promised return with spring.
Time pasts, months come and gone,
She still awaits the new dawn.
Her summer smile wanes,
Flora withers to Autumn's stains.
Speckled tears bleed orange and red,
Flora, her subject's solemn, dead.
Winter chills from Nature's heartbreak,
Trailing snows in her wake.
Season, her colorful king,
Handsomely riding, trumpeting spring.
Season tends to death's neglect,
Worshiping Flora bows in respect.
Mother Nature's heart warmed,
Her Kingdom transformed.

By Lisa Hiatt

Jesus In A Box

With all the Christmas bustle the holiday cheer,
Is sometimes forgotten this time of year
I hate the shopping the stores overflow,
People bickering where ever you go.
As I walked fuming from a store,
There in a wheelchair sat a child by the door
She looked about six, a box clutched in her little grasp,
Looking so like this gift was her last.
She smiled her secret smile and offered it to me,
I opened the box, it was… Empty?
I frowned not understanding the prize,
Slowly hurt showed in her big blue eyes.
She softly spoke her little voice like a sigh,
"Don't you get it?" Her sweet lisped reply.
I shook my head, my puzzlement showed,
Minute by minute I felt like a toad.
"I gave you Jesus in this little box."
That nearly knocked off my socks.
"See, he is the gift and the reason,
For all to celebrate this season.
So this gift I share, it's true,
Belongs to someone like you."
My surliness faded as I look on,
She had the answers all along.
I felt humbled by her gift she shared,
My tears falling I wasn't prepared.
I took her gift, kissing her brow.
And on that day I made a solemn vow.
To treat Christmas as a lesson retrieved,
Relishing in the special gift received

By Lisa Hiatt

Collector

You're a collector I see,
You and your eccentricity.
Stamps, trinkets, ancient books,
Keep your snobby dirty looks.
I am a collector too it would seem,
More precious then you could ever dream.
I be a collector of souls,
Find that in your moldy scrolls.
My collection puts all yours to shame,
In death it's I who calls your name.
I who collects your light,
Turning brightness to night.
So shiver in your boots you pitiful fool,
In this world I rule.

By Lisa Hiatt

Midsummer's Eve

Once upon a midsummer's eve,
Woven magic for those that believe.
Glittering stars speckle the ebony skies,
Dancing fairies in the darkness arise.
Wings beat a gentle breeze,
Tickling the nose to make a sneeze.
Fairy dust brushes summer air,
Trailing sprinkles everywhere.
For the moment winter is lost,
Slumber sweetly Jack Frost.
Dancing and giggling the night away,
Trees and flora gently sway.
Crickets chirp a snappy tune,
Aglow by the light of the harvest moon.
Iridescent wings of azure blue,
Ushering morning luminously anew.
Sleep now fairies by dawns early light,
Evening comes soon for fanciful flight.

By Lisa Hiatt

Heavenly

Ebony canvas fireflies alight,
Sparkling gems a little past midnight.
Respite from worry and sorrow,
Secure with promises of tomorrow.
Footprints on brown-sugar sand,
Hand in hand, in slumber-land.
Wrinkled toes in azure seas,
Emerald leaves on humorous trees.
Cotton-candy afloat on honeysuckle air,
Gates barred from loneliness and despair.
Dawning egg in over-easy skies,
Wishes granted upon magenta sunrise.
Content for now, rest deep,
Dream while you can in heavenly sleep.

By Lisa Hiatt

Winter Bliss

Smooth, cool dark chocolate night,
Swiss cheese moon illuminating light.
Marshmallows dot the ebony canvas,
Fondued decadent bliss.
Mars basking in the Milky Way,
Snowman wants to play.
Pretzel-ed branches beseech,
Spring just out of reach.
Powdered sugar peppers coffeed ground,
Ivory scenery profound.
Whipped cream peaked pine,
Delectably divine.
Squirrels busy with winter stow,
Putting on quite a show.
Popsicles decorate the eave,
Jack Frost's magical weave.
Snowbirds enjoy vacation from heat,
Ah winter wonderland so sweet.

By Lisa Hiatt

Obscure Dreams

Luminous countenance obscurity awaits,
Dusk contemplates.
Engorged sphere rests in celestial stillness,
Enlightening the unwillingness.
Amber glow come forth boldly bright,
Keep company the iridescent stars tonight.
The patterned heaven holds a fairy-tale,
Baptized with holy Braille.
Calling forth Aurora Borealis,
Illuminated chilled spatial palace.
Dancing through time on lunar-beams,
Within unfulfilled prophetic dreams.

By Lisa Hiatt

Love's Demise

Thou heart but fickle hath no appeal,
Holder of blood scarlet surreal.
Deep in mine chest a feeble beat,
Love finds unblissful retreat.
A time long ago twin beats as one,
Mine soul withers from actions done.
Betrayer thou lips bereaved kiss,
Thine so cold with absence bliss.
Grieving for love's demise,
Mine heart burdened with unshed good-byes.

By Lisa Hiatt

Within The Darkness

Within the darkness I can write,
My soul fills with the light.
Within the darkness I can cry,
No one knows I long to die.

Within the darkness I write of despair,
Others sometimes don't really care.
Within the darkness echoes hollow empathy,
Empty promises of how they care for me.

Within the darkness I lose hope,
Watching the hangman's rope.
Within the darkness is my inner child,
My loving father defiled.

Within the darkness lives a fear,
That God isn't really here.
That loneliness and despair,
Will always remain there.

Within this darkness shines a light,
A poet's heart will always write.
Within the darkness I'll survive,
The writer in me keeps me alive.

By Lisa Hiatt

Tears Of Pearl

Tears of pearl dew drop rain,
Falling down her cheeks stain.
The darkness conceals her plight,
Crying in the ebony night.
The moon aglow within the tears,
Bitter sorrow for all the years.
Wasted on a hopeless cause,
Blinded by his many flaws.
The silence is filled,
With love unfulfilled.
Chills of the ebony night,
Embeds within her heart's plight.
Soon pearl drops turn to ice,
Hardened from her sacrifice.
Cold winter chills her heart,
A safe guard from love's dart.
Tears of pearls like a necklace worn,
Glowing like the moon forlorn.
Cold against her skin,
Like the ice cubes within.
He swore he'd never go astray,
But he did anyway.
So like her teardrops made of ice,
Her heart paid the price.
Maybe someday she'll find bliss,
With another's kiss.
But for now her heart encased,
Heartache is such a waste.
You can keep love at bay,
But somehow it will find you anyway.

By Lisa Hiatt

Moondust

Moondust aglow,
Speckles light as snow.
Capture a moonbeam,
Like an elusive dream.
Beams glowing pale,
Cold luminous trail.
Holding illusions within grasp,
Ebbing like times past.
Love is compared to the moon,
Burning brightly, ending too soon.
Fleeting like starlight,
Thriving in the dark of night.
Does true love exist?
Or just a midnight tryst?
Emotions fleeting like lust,
Nah, it is only Moondust.

By Lisa Hiatt

Blue Goddess

Blue moon on the rise,
A reflection of her eyes.
Stars sparkle on her ebony gown,
Aurora Borealis in her wake trailing down.
Celestial palace her domain,
The galaxy worships her name.
Heartlessly cold,
Timelessly old.
Holder of the night,
Keeper of starlight.
Her beauty captured beyond the moon,
Morning awakens too soon.
In daylight she sleeps,
The evening weeps.
She dreams of her celestial palace,
The Milky Way her chalice.
The belle of the ball,
Planets at her beck and call.
The stars enlighten heaven's floor,
Calling her to shine once more.

By Lisa Hiatt

Sun God

The sun the fire in his eyes,
Azure robes are in the skies.
He sits in the daylight throne,
Pining for a lover of his own.
Looking towards the moonlit sky,
Forlorn with a mournful sigh.
He knows she lives by night,
And he is keeper of the light.
She the moon in ebony skies,
He the sun at sunrise.
So he guards her by day,
While she sleeps the light away.
And she guards his light,
Until the end of night.
He tries to hand her a bouquet,
But alas it's just a touch away.

By Lisa Hiatt

Beast

What is that sound upon my windowpane,
Is it the sound of the dreary rain?
Then why does my heart strum a tempoed beat,
Why has fear not found retreat?
A chuckle at my paranoid ways,
Choking with discovery of amber gaze.
Sharp claws are tapping, scratching at the glass,
My heart beats ever, ever so fast.
Me thinks I'm safe behind four walls
An eerie howl, my skin crawls.
Hot breath fogs the cool glass,
Images evoked of my skin slashed.
Of sharp teeth biting through sinew and flesh,
Predictions of my emanate death.
I wake to the sound of a crunching bone,
Realization dawning, they're my own.

By Lisa Hiatt

Moon Rose

Moon-kissed rose amber light,
Glowing in the ebony night.
Dew drops grace petals tender,
Sweet scented night surrender.
Softly she sings a mournful plight,
So lonely in the ebony night.
Her thorns fall forlorn to the ground,
Echoing in the silence found.
She mourns for her lover the moon,
His distance hard to attune.
Her petals limp in his glowing light,
So lost in the ebony night.
His glow so pale,
That she's so frail.
Shivering in the moonlight,
She sings of her mournful plight.
The sun with his fire awakes,
Watching his heart breaks.
Shining down to warm her heart,
Wanting to be a special part.
Radiant with a warming light,
She gives up the moonlit night.
Now her lover is sunshine.
Their love so divine.

By Lisa Hiatt

Raven

Comes the raven dark and leery,
Heralding death so dreary.
Perched on fading tombstone,
The owner unknown.
Oily black his feather shine,
He's telling me I'm out of time.
Echoing through still solemn trees,
Prayers unanswered on my knees.
The clock chimes the witching hour,
From his obscure shadow I cower.
I beg the raven for more time,
Beady eyes judge me for my crime.
Comes death with his foggy wake,
I pray my soul the Lord will take.
Pointing his emaciated finger of bone,
Etching my name on the tombstone.

By Lisa Hiatt

Within

Darkness within,
Deep under the skin.
Blood scarlet surreal,
Layers of deceit conceal.
Wrong choices made,
Enjoyment of games played.
Freewill to choose,
Wrong one, you lose.

By Lisa Hiatt

Tremors

With trepidation held the trembling bird,
Gentling her with kindness and soft word.
Breast bruised from heightened fall,
Caged heart silenced her beauteous call.
She trembles under thou tender care,
She so lost in obscure despair.
With time her voice sang,
Happiness and joy rang.
Her heart vibrates with love,
Spreading ivory wings of a dove.
To have a love meant to be,
Thou must set her free.
Taking flight she soars,
Back into thou arms, I am yours.

By Lisa Hiatt

The Dragon

I saw in my father's eyes the beast arising,
Like a mighty dragon it reared its ugly head.
The hate hypnotizing,
Filling my little heart with dread.

He smiles evilly with his sharp toothy grin,
His large paws heavily descend.
I close my eyes hiding the fear within,
Wishing with all my might for a hero to defend.

What had I done that warranted his wrath,
The blows that came had drawn first blood.
The marks left behind made a scaring path
I climbed to my little feet again in the gory crud.

Now as a parent I have become the slayer,
I have slain the mighty dragon called abuse.
I teach my children years later,
Hurting others is just an excuse.

Climb bravely to your feet,
And present the other cheek.
Abuse will find defeat,
The dragon is battered and weak.

By Lisa Hiatt

Scarlet Thorn

The thorn lances deep in my skin,
Scarlet flows from within.
Blood soaked petals softly tender,
Lovingly exquisite I surrender.
I offer my heart this red rose,
With words sweet as a lovers prose.
Bleeding words with love's stain,
Engraved calligraphy on my brain.
Blood scented as red rose,
As unfathomable, as it flows.
A drop of blood drips down,
To soak the parched ground.
And in its place grows,
The scarlet red rose.
Hold close this wild bouquet,
Do not hasten to give it away.
For love is fragrantly divine,
Nectar as sweet as red wine.

By Lisa Hiatt

Between

The house stood in the wheat field,
With broken shutters and paint peeled.
Aimless among the rows of gold,
The door creeps open an invitation from the cold.
A single candle lit in front of faded window sheers,
The sky fat with unshed tears.
Shadows seem to crowd the night,
Dancing across the candle light.
Frigid wind blows on by,
Wheat shafts bow beneath the sky.
Cracks and creaks shutter's mourn,
A lonely melody sadly forlorn.
Gloomy withstanding the elements outside,
Crestfallen like the grain farmer's pride.
Aimless among the wheat field,
With broken shutters and paint peeled.
The barn disgraced with disrepair,
Like hopes lost to despair.
Abandoned building crumbling like a dream,
Bewildered like the nightmares in between.

By Lisa Hiatt

Color Blind

My world just stopped its color today,
Watched it turn shades of gray.
Though life goes on I'm color blind,
My heart lays abandon, love left behind.
Frosty breaths, the air cold as ice,
Chest bleeds from a wide open slice.
Torn loose from tissue and sinew,
An act done from love untrue.
Palms cradle a beating heart,
A gift returned since you had a part.
Blood drips through numb finger tips,
As chilled as the frigid smile on lips.
Soul lays dormant the conscience sleeps,
Killing you softly for each tear that weeps.
Shattered heart shards of broken glass,
Fall to the ground like love from the past.
Hold head high just turn and walk away,
Always felt partial to shades of gray.

By Lisa Hiatt

My Hero, My Daughter

Though your battle's been waged,
Your strength's be gauged.
I have learned a lesson my little one,
Your courage is more bravely done.
The cancer might have taken a part,
But you've shown me your lion-heart.
Climbing mountains with one hand,
You won't be labeled with a handicapped brand.
Teaching me self-pity's for fools,
Showing you can live by your own rules.
Your kindness shown steadfast and true,
Even after all you've been through.
I love you so, come hell or high water,
My Hero, My daughter.

By Lisa Hiatt

Bob

Dawn of the dead,
Rest your sweet head.
Polluted tide will rock you,

Rest assured,
It can't be cured.
The water's no longer blue.

Hothouse flower,
Acid rain shower.
Skin turns to ash,

There's no alarm,
It has its charm.
Before you, life'll flash.

So with gurgling sound,
You will drown.
Buoyancy is a fine job,

Tides go out, so like trash,
Please don't feel abash.
We can always rename you Bob.

By Lisa Hiatt

Fool

O what a fool am I,
Of this I do not deny.
Mine heart but a painted clown,
Mine laughter but a frown.
I but a mortal be,
Thou but a bird, set free.
Thy wings took flight,
Vanishing into the night.
O how mine heart'll bleed,
Of thine betrayal it would not heed.
For even after the deed be done,
I be the foolish one.
Thou promised love such splendor,
Of mine love I did surrender.
I gave up mine foolish heart,
Tears falling as thou depart.
I played a risky game,
I be part to blame.
I was a foolish fool,
Thou be the most cruel.
I knew the chance I'd take,
And end with the heartbreak.
But thou such a beauteous bird,
I believed in thine words whispered.
I believed thou would return,
But alas I inhabit love's burn.
Thou be wild and free,
Thou will n'er return to me.

By Lisa Hiatt

Bayou

Rock lazy harvest moon gently velvet night,
Twinkling stars celestial bedtime-light.
Moonbeams glowing gingerbread sweet,
Honeysuckle winds blow down Bourbon Street.
Tambourine branches shake the leaves,
Night alive with magical weaves
Harvest reflection in the river's wake,
Rippling soothingly each breath it'll take.
Crickets chirp Blue Danube,
Frogs keep tempo in the Bayou.
Fireflies dance all abright,
While harvest moon yawns good-night.

By Lisa Hiatt

Baby Boy

Rock so sweetly my wee one,
Gently dream of your deeds done.
Chasing dragons and fairy tales,
With snips, snails and puppy dog tails.
Your world so small within your grasp,
Sweet hours that fly past.
Of truck, trailer and other toy,
My darling child, my little boy.
Magic worlds you will find,
While your dreams unwind.
Sleep my little son sleep,
Little shepherd count sheep.
I softly kiss your sweet brow,
On this starry night I make a vow.
I promise you my little one,
You my most precious son.
Stars may fall from heavens sky,
Years may rapidly fly by.
You my pride and joy,
Will always be my baby boy.

By Lisa Hiatt

Baby Girl

My baby girl my first born child,
Wonders shown the moment you smiled.
Keeper of my lonely heart,
You became that special part.
From the first day you came,
You held my heart's flame.
With your giggles so sweet,
You made my life complete.
When I first felt your kicking,
I also felt my heart quickening.
I knew soon you'd be born,
I felt so lost my firstborn.
I didn't feel like I could care for you.
As much as I needed to,
But you showed me my little one.
You loved me in spite of what I've done,
Now you've grown right in front of me.
And showed me your inner beauty.
I am so proud of you my little girl,
You made a place for yourself in this world.

By Lisa Hiatt

Valentine's Day

It's not the cards and candy that make true love
It's the way we snuggle and fit like a glove.
It's when you brush my hair gently with every stroke,
Not the flowers clogging allergies which make me choke.
It's when you clip my toenails I no longer reach,
Or when I need suntan oil on that spot at the beach
I know you don't have a romantic bone,
But you always SHOW you care for me when we're all alone.
You tell me how you love me only, for my cooking,
Always taking seconds when you think I'm not looking.
It's when you laugh when I break a little wind,
Forgiving for the smell and me so chagrined.
You've never been too keen at showing love for all to see,
But you always SHOW me you care for me.
You don't always tell me, "I love you,"
You always SHOW me what's true.
So with Valentine's Day just around the bend,
I don't expect anything that you may send
I've the trust and know how you're very true blue,
Even if you look at other girls at least a time two,
Though I know it's not true.
You tell me, "I only look to compare them to you."
I'm content in knowing I'll have you all my life,
And someday soon I'll be your wife.
Valentine's Day has it own meaning to me anyway,
That your love's deep even if it isn't in romantic words you say.
Home's where the heart is, the saying very true,
House maintenance is never overdue.
You're always there for me when I need a house so strong,
You're MY HOME and where I'll always belong.

What Valentine's Day means to me, Happy Valentine's Day Charles Cooper all my love Lisa!

By Lisa Hiatt

Broken Rose

Sharp thorn pierces skin,
Blood flows from within.
Blade sharp as steel,
Turbulent emotions surreal.
Watching as it wells and drips,
Onto ice cold lips.
My sanity gone,
I don't think I had it all along.
My heart pumps,
With dull thumps.
Counting down till the last beat,
As I lay dying at your feet.
Words unspoken freeze in my brain,
I ponder the absence of pain.
Floating through time and space,
How I long to see your face.
One more time before I go,
And you don't even know.
Bleeding so divine,
Like a poison Ivy vine.
Such beauty in death,
I take my last breath.
Colder and colder still,
Love broken against my will.
The rose like wild thorn,
Sharply reborn.
I am wrapped in barbed vine,
Reborn chilled what was mine.
Drained of crimson red,
Conceived undead.
Pluck not my rose,
I pierce and blood flows.
Warm on fingertips,
Caught on eager lips.

By Lisa Hiatt

Whispering Wolf

Come ne'er to still woods and fear,
The silence ne'er golden here.
When the moon be full,
Ye be feelin' the pull.
The whisper of the beast,
On thine bones will feast.
Come ne'er at full of moon,
Hear the lonely croon.
Thine bones but a midnight snack,
He comes in shadows black.
None in harbor safe for he come,
Thrill of the kill please run.
Feasting on blood and gore,
Sharp razor talon's score.
Whispering wolf come,
He hears thine heart drum.
He smiles with an evil grin,
Enjoying the sin.
The gory thrill,
Of the sacrificial kill.
So come if ye dare,
I but meet thou there.

By Lisa Hiatt

New England

Rocking on the water's tide,
Midnight lazing lullabye ride.
Full moon on the rise,
In velvet chocolate smooth skies.
Jasmine fills the whispering breeze,
Lethargic rustles in the trees.
A wolf howls a lonely tune,
A serenade to the shining moon.
Crickets chirp a tempoed beat,
Tickling rapids trailing feet.
Sweet clover rests between lips,
Fishing pole loose in fingertips.
O I think I have a bite,
Just jump on board, too languid to fight.
low hung sneaky stars within a grip,
a wish made before they slip.
Like fireflies enlightening the bay,
Rocking me to the Milky Way.

By Lisa Hiatt

Lotus Blossom

She like the willow weeps,
As the passage of time creeps.
Apple blossoms tears fall,
Jasmine scented dreams call.
A gown of lotus blossom white,
She dressed for the ball that night.
Butterflies adorned her hair,
She awaits her warrior there.
The bridge over waters so still,
With rose vines tendril.
The beauty couldn't break her despair,
Her warrior wasn't there.
Midnight came and went,
Her blossom tears spent.
Fragile broken hearted,
She lifted her lotus gown and departed.
Her warrior gone to war,
Had promised like many times before.
That She was his one and only,
But his nights were so lonely.
So He took another each town,
War took him around.
Lotus blossom don't cry,
Somehow you'll get by.
Remember this,
You'll find love in another's kiss.

By Lisa Hiatt

Afterglow

Drunk on tempered lips,
Shivers from cool fingertips.
Sweet wine the taste divine,
Tickling tongues intertwine.
Lovers embrace like rose tendrilling,
The scent of afterglow fulfilling.
The world unheard,
Lost in words whispered.
Silence is golden like the moonshine,
This place of yours and mine.

By Lisa Hiatt

The Shortcut

A shortcut through the trees,
The smell of wet fur on the breeze
Whispers in the dark,
Shadows leaving an oily mark
The walk down the path
Where the leaves dance a wrath
Over shadows on the lane,
The wind cold with stinging pain
I try to hum under my breath,
And not think of death
I hasten my pace,
To end this death race
Shadows are chasing me,
Over every rock, and bush I see.
The path seems to glow,
And the length to grow.
With each step I take,
Lungs are about to break.
The world stands still,
As I reach the steep hill,
Branches reaching out,
To upend my route.
I would feel so warm,
Safe out of this storm
If I could only reach,
My house by the beach.
My breath begins to wheeze,
As I breathe the musky breeze
And when I look back,
I see amber eyes shrouded in black
With teeth as sharp as nail,
Fears of my emanate impale.
I make it to my door,
With relief, I swore.
I reach out to open the lock,
And imagine the shock,
As two furry taloned paws,
Pulls me to razored jaws.

By Lisa Hiatt

Taste for Blood

Heady smell thickly intense,
Just a taste against all common sense.
Scarlet cascade down it flows,
Like soft petals of a rose.
Plucked fill the satin sheet,
The smell floral sweet.
The taste for blood overwhelms,
Carrying me off to other realms.
Sharp sabers press against skin,
The mind filled with wicked sin.
Eyes of amber light,
Glowing embers bright.
Like a moth caught in twin flames,
Vigilant as the essence drains.
Slumber sweetly my lover,
Amorous night sumptuous to discover.

By Lisa Hiatt

Thread

Like a thread spun with pristine gold,
Some lives existing until we grow old.
Longer, stronger when we are young,
On silver spindles we are strung.
With age comes some wisdom I fear,
Not all will reside here.
For the three fates,
Have a say what life dictates.
With platinum scissors sharp as a knife,
Cutting short even the most glorious life.
The thread of life is precious to hold,
Like a thread spun with pristine gold.

By Lisa Hiatt

Beauty in Death

Even scarlet roses bloom,
In obscure cemetery gloom.
The mournful night weep…
For scented rose deep.
Basking in full moon's glow,
Silhouetted trees worship beauty below.
Even sweet roses share,
While solemnly residing there.
For in somber gloom,
Is the splendor of the bloom.
Finding beauty in all thou see,
Roses within art the beauty of thee.

By Lisa Hiatt

Fallen angels

Keepers of the night,
Of the stars holy light.
Wrapped with golden wings,
And mercy the Lord brings.
We sheep, his fallen one,
For us given his only son.
God with his graceful love,
Sent angels from above.
To shepherd his sheep,
From death's endless sleep.
Guiding to heaven's door,
To shine on paradise's floor.
Ebony canvas in earthly night,
Twinkling with the star's holy light.

By Lisa Hiatt

Archangel

O me but a mortal bespelled,
In purgatory dwelled.
An ardent lover's kiss.

Mine battered heart found,
Mine soul a new prison bound.
Pain holds no bliss.

Thou gently tamed the bitter tear,
Love lost resided here
I long for thou tender embrace

Thy satin ties that bind,
So easily unwind.
Rescued from heaven's disgrace.

Archangel slayer of foolish pride,
Found the tenderness hidden inside.
Thou hold the key,

So ardent lover I bid thee,
Hold fast mine bruised heart gently.
Thou hast set me free.

By Lisa Hiatt

Yesterday

Dust devils dance on furrowed space,
Aged tears fall staining his face.
So many years spent working the land,
The dry dust slips from his wrinkled hand.
Abandoned buildings crumbling like dreams.
The tears flow in streams.
Memories of long ago from a distant past,
Stay just out of his grasp.
He bows his head in defeat,
The breeze kicking up dust at his feet.
If only youth would have held on a little longer,
If only he was a little stronger.
"Come on pop it's time to go."
He calls back without turning, "I know."
With age comes progress life goes on,
Even after the memories are gone.
Though his heart feels sorrow,
He turns and departs, there is always tomorrow.

By Lisa Hiatt

Breach

Dark knight upon pale steed,
Why for hath thee considered mine plead.
I but a maiden lost in silent thought,
Hath thee grown weary of battles fought.
Doth mine humble presence amuse thee?
Or art thou bespelled by mine beauty?
Noble knight I beseech,
Do not mine maidhood breach.
I would be unsuitable for another's embrace,
A fallen angel, from heaven's disgrace.
Dare I see an evil glint in thee obscure eye?
The rewards too immense to deny?
I give of mine self freely, I ask but one demand,
Petition from father, for mine hand.
Thou mock with cruel laughter,
I but lost from here after.
Mine barren heart slowly dies,
Thou mocking laughter so chastise.
Art thou heart so hardened to loves breach?
Thou soul so cold to love's reach?
I disturb thee, I speak no more,
Deafness falls from mine implore.
Guard thou heart with cruelty,
For I only feel pity.
Thou heart may keep from loves breach,
But mine love, is out of thou reach.
Thou may breach mine maidhood by battle's won,
But I be the stronger one.

By Lisa Hiatt

Looking Glass

Breath fogs the looking glass,
Watching the world's teaming mass.
On the outside looking in,
Wanting to be part is such a sin.
Face pressed against broken glass,
Touching reality is just out of my grasp.
Kept a prisoner against my will,
My only company the mirror's chill.
I fight my demons that keep me here,
With loneliness and repressed tear.
I so long for a valiant knight,
To win this battle that I must fight.
Riding up on his white steed,
To quench this overwhelming need.
This looking glass that I dwell,
My fear, this everlasting hell.

By Lisa Hiatt

Destroying Angel

The world keeps turning in black and white,
As the craziness turns hold sanity tight.
Polluting the children, no respect learned,
Abuse ramped nothing earned.
Close your eyes let it slip away,
Cover your ears to the words I say.
Obscurity conceals techno colored world,
Demonic wings unfurled.
Destroying angel, gentle sensual smile,
The world will be mine....in a while.

By Lisa Hiatt

Chained

Cloaked in darkness chained,
Heartbreak has left me restrained.
This prison keeps my heart,
From sharing that part.
The chains that guard,
Are welded hard.
A sacrifice for love's demise,
Weary of so many good-byes.
Your armor shines bright,
My valiant white knight.
With gentle care,
Rescued me from despair.
Freed from chain that binds,
Unlocked only true love unwinds.
So hold gently I bid my knight,
For only your love makes it right.

By Lisa Hiatt

Crimson Tide

Words of kindness easily spill,
Like rain upon the windowsill.
Kindness n'er reaches amber eyes,
Benevolent evil in disguise.
Nails of diamond scrape chilled skin,
Boundless darkness lurks within.
Hold screams tight in the throat,
Crimson rain, sacrificial goat.
Rasping breath like fetid meat,
Too tardy now for safe retreat.
Darkness o'er takes the vacant stare,
Descending fangs reflected there.
Light grows dim from depths so bright,
A greedy lapping in the night.
Heady smells of crimson tide,
Weariness penetrates deep inside.
Sanity slips away like rain,
Pattering on the windowpane.

By Lisa Hiatt

Fairies

Holes dot the Mason jar lid,
Nocturnal fey stay hid.
The firefly dances around bespelled eyes,
Crafty fairies in disguise.
Tinkling laughter with a miss,
Reaching out to capture one's wish.
Contented children spin around,
Like falling leaves to the ground.
Summer magic but an enchanted spell,
Like sparkling fairy-dust dispel.
Soon the call to march on home,
Leaving mischievous fairies alone.
Painting the sky with stars so bright,
Shining down, shimmering in the ebony night.

By Lisa Hiatt

Bloodred

Pity slips through death's fingers like sand,
In the ocean of lost souls greed holds his hand.
The dawn born bloodred,
The wind moans the song of the dead.
War watches with its greedy eyes,
Hope swallows the lump she cries.
Love sleeps somewhere in the distance,
As if it would make a difference.
Over the moaning starvation cackles his hysterical laugh,
Vultures play out his wraith.
The end is near,
The angel of mercy is here.
She turns her head,
She won't mourn the valiant soldier's dead.
She bestows wings,
To the children caught in the middle of things.
This evil rules the heart of man,
Grasped tightly in death's hand.

By Lisa Hiatt

Rose Child

Hold soft a rose, gently use,
For too harsh and it may bruise.
Compare a child to red rose,
The petals fall so easily with bitter blows.
The child will grow like the flower to bare,
Thorns that prick and thoughts of little care.
Hold fast in truth, bitter words take root,
Like weeds in the garden soil and soot.
Spreading wild unless tamed with love,
With gentle patience and sun from above.
The warmth caresses the blushing cheek,
While thriving in the warmth it'll seek.
Though rain may fall to wash away,
Some bitter tears may stay.
Hold close the rose and cherish its beauty,
Each one to tend a parent's duty.
Remember though this rose child,
Isn't always so loud and wild.
For they too need a tender caress,
To bring out their very best.

By Lisa Hiatt

Rainbow

My artisan came and colored my world,
With multicolored hues swirled.
My heart, entwined ebony rose,
The love encased never grows.
Thorns had embedded its prickly spine,
Wrapped in pain the love that was mine.
Within the wake of dreary despair,
I forgot that your love was always there.
You my artisan with passion stroked,
A rainbow for a heart tendril choked.
My heart etched with devotion so true,
With colors so dazzling just for you.

By Lisa Hiatt

The Auction

Sad eyes watch as her memories are sold,
The auctioneer's voice rings out fast and cold.
She tries to reach out and grasp her treasure,
To that one memory that gave her pleasure.
Alas, the memory slips through her transparent hand,
Confusion crosses her sad eyes, she can't comprehend.
She beseeches an on looker, "Sir, please listen to me,
Why must you buy my memories?"
For a moment he looks as if he heard,
But sadly he heard not a word.
She swallows a lump; a voice stops her retreat,
"You no longer live on this street."
"It's time to come home," an angel replies,
Gently wiping the tears from her eyes.
She looks up, smiling and taking his outstretched hands,
With humble radiance, she now understands.
She turns back for one last look, to say her good-byes,
Taking flight towards heaven she flies.

By Lisa Hiatt

Witness

Within fleshy walls exists a retched soul,
Which heartache has taken its toll.
You may look upon and see,
How blankness looks back at thee.
Her eyes but cold mercury glass,
Long ago abandon from abuse in the past.
Her father stole the innocence there,
From a heart that once she'd freely share.
You may look upon with pity and shame,
But she exists with this pain.
She carries this burden like a generous broach,
Pinned to her breast witnessed at approach.
To be kind you shy away,
Not quite sure what you'd say.
To comment would mean,
You have witnessed her heartache's scene.
So you walk away,
It's easier than words you'd say.
For if you look too deeply in her eyes,
It may be your reflection, in disguise.

By Lisa Hiatt

Eyes Wide Closed

With youth the heart opens wide,
Room for love to step inside.
Bittersweet it lasted only a moment in time,
Eyes closed now from the radiant shine.
Not wanting to open again no room for more,
Not willing to open love's door.
Morally unbending the risk too great,
Not willing to share the bittersweet hate.
Two sides of the coin but one in the same,
Finding no cause or the other to blame.
You feel you have given it a try,
But closed your soul will slowly die.
Yes it's true you won't feel pain,
From loves bittersweet stain.
But closed eyes draw the moth to the flame,
Seeking out your heart to whisper their name.

By Lisa Hiatt

Tears of Stone

Ice-cubes dance in whiskey glass,
Oscillating rings flow to hand grasp.
Shattering the silence with effervescent tune,
Resonating in the heart's heavy gloom.
A pickled self-centered soul,
With a wasted goal.
Melancholy to the very bone.
Finding comfort in the tinkling tone.
Sorrow drowning in whiskey glass,
Painted smile on a clown's mask.
Hide the feelings like shame,
No one wants to see the pain.
Harden the heart no feelings shown,
Till you cry tears of stone.

Origami

My fragile heart like Origami,
Carefully folded a creation of beauty.
Intricate folds a scarlet rose,
Within the dark recesses it glows.
So fragile is my paper heart,
Braving love though easily torn apart.
To capture my heart of solid gold,
Love comes quickly; it's not easy to hold.
The price too high to give your all,
And some don't want to truly fall.
I only ask one thing of you,
Give love that's only true.
Don't give my heart empty lies,
Or complicated good-byes.
Within the folds of my paper heart,
Lays an endless supply of love as a part.
My love freely given with no strings,
And all the joys that love brings.

By Lisa Hiatt

My Heart

Cradled in my palms to see,
My heart beating back at me.
With the seconds that tick by,
You can't count the tears I cry.
The beats get fainter with passage of time,
Slower still as the clock'll chime.
Bury me not with this gaping hole,
Give your love filling my heart and soul.
Glue together which was once broke,
Stitch love into every stroke.
When you mend every part,
That is when I give you my heart.

By Lisa Hiatt

Over the Rise

Aussie tumbleweeds across the dry dirt,
Sweat parched on cowhand's shirt.
Unrelenting sun beats down on the brain,
Unanswered prayers to the gods of rain.
Blessed river refreshing to the withering heat,
Waters rushing across the rocks so sweet.
Stealthy cattle just out of site,
Sun still heats with the coming of night.
Cowboy hat brim brings no relief,
Though the ending day will be brief.
A coyote howl sings out soft and low,
Horse's progress is labored and slow.
Wiping dust from squinting eyes,
I just know the cattle are over that rise.

By Lisa Hiatt

Cocoon

Soft petals on spring flora sealed,
Bursting forth colors splendor grassy field.
Warm winds blowing the meadow dances,
While birds sing sweet romances.
Wrapped in ivory, silky, cozy cocoon,
Squirming anticipation transforming very soon.
Magical embrace by sweet mother earth,
Gifting homely caterpillar with rebirth.
The present opens one fine morn,
Beautiful butterfly awakens reborn.

By Lisa Hiatt

Moon

O beguiling moon on which I gaze,
Of your iridescence I do praise.
My heart but a mortal beat,
Upon your silent strength I seek.
Your beauty captures my presence,

Try as I may I cannot see,
Why the glow enchants me.
For it is but an iridescent light,
Full, round and bright.
I'm but an insect caught in the essence.

I've gazed in wonder,
Transfixed under.
Show me the way,
Selene, enlighten my way.
Grant me your silent strength,

Your magic is an illusion,
To fill hearts with confusion.
And I'm but a fool,
finding the gods to be cruel.
I need understanding at any length.

By Lisa Hiatt

Selene's Moon

O Selene, upon this enchanted night,
Spherical, engorged and bright.
I but a remote maiden worship thee,
Thou heavenly glow beckons me.
Liberate me from mine errant plight,
Sentinel of the darkened night.
Thou luminous glow bespells,
Within mine soul desolation dwells
Send me but a honorable knight,
To amend mine forlorn plight.
Keeper of ancient secrets see,
How solitary a maiden I be.
I wish upon thou celestial light,
For thine divine guidance tonight.
Harden not thou beauteous heart,
For I beseech for love's amorous dart.

By Lisa Hiatt

Daisies Fair

Petals soft scent lingers,
Pollen gold upon the fingers.
Petals ivory sailing down,
Gently falling to the ground.
He loves me, but a few petals away,
Tongue peeks through lips in determined way.
My breath held for the last tug,
He loves me not, I only shrug.
The meadow full of daisies fair,
I'll eventually find the right answer there.

By Lisa Hiatt

Unleash

Unleash the tides of fury unto the sea,
Keep the waters rising endlessly.
Thou titan of the waters black,
Hold not thine fury back.
Sink ships low to their watery grave,
Though still they sail the foolishly brave.
Mermaids serenade mariner buffoons,
Send them to their watery tombs.
A sailor spirited mine heart from me,
His love was only for Mistress Sea.
So unleash thine fury o titan Poseidon,
I n'er see mine lover again.
I glimpse clouds gather o'er the sea,
Carry not mine lover back to me.
I curse his soul to a watery grave,
Though mine heart be his devoted slave.
Mine tears of salt keep bitter seas so deep,
While he doth with the fishes sleep.

By Lisa Hiatt

Floral Rain

Me thinks oh lover of floral rain,
Cometh thus swiftly with love's stain,
Enlighten me with roses so sweet,
Laying petals at mine feet.
Thou essence fills thee with fragrant poem,
Bestowed upon me and the garden gnome.
Sweetly thou words quicken mine heart,
Impaling swiftly with love's sharp dart.
Inhaling beauty of thine bouquet,
Treasured always thine words thou say.
So dear lover meet by garden stair,
Thou scented rose will await thee there.
Mine sweet lover find reverence in this,
Me wilt bequeath thee a chaste kiss.
Thou lip as sweet as a nosegay of rose,
Sweeter still thine words of prose.

By Lisa Hiatt

Jester

What a fool, my mortal soul, bleed,
It mourns with aching need.
What humiliation does my jester's heart laugh,
A bitter sound as thorny love drives a pointed shaft.
Can I be but saved,
Or imprisoned, adoration enslaved.
I beckon to the Goddess of peace,
Make this infernal pain cease.
But yet my heart, drones its beat,
The sorrow finds no retreat.

By Lisa Hiatt

Azure

Cold granite marks the spot,
Luminous green grass the plot,
Icy fingers crush daisies she'd love.

Gray clouds cover azure blue,
My heart screams, I miss you,
Her eyes matched the azure above.

Rain soaked tears slide down pale cheeks,
Laughter echoes in silent streets.
The breeze mourns, she was once there.

I held her hand, she slipped from me,
Now only, her bright memory.
Skin soaked, too numb to care.

Crushed yellow daisies float down,
slowly to the wet ground.
A promise, I will return,
Emotions churn,

Tomorrow is another day,
I still have more to say.
Clouds part, azure shines through,
As if to say, I'll miss you too.

By Lisa Hiatt

Craven

Craven knight on battle field's fought,
Why so distraught?
As the battle wages all around,
Why not thou courage be found.
Thou knees quake so as armors chime,
The advancing foe so prime.
They only to follow echoing din,
To find thou secreted within.
You may hide from thine foe in obscurity,
But from thine own-self there be no security.
Thou may go through life with trepidations intact,
But thou n'er win honor back.

By Lisa Hiatt

The Doll

She lay broken this little porcelain doll,
Her tear stained face turned to the wall.
Angry words fall shattering her soul,
His blows finally took their toll.
With one last shallow exhale,
He drove her last coffin nail.
Porcelain doll broken by a coward so cruel,
For his sin branded the worst kind of fool.
Like any fool, he didn't learn from his mistake,
With his actions he has sealed his own fate.
In prison the inmates have a justice for his kind,
Proving that justice isn't blind.
Now the coward lay like a broken doll,
His shattered body turned to the wall.

By Lisa Hiatt

Poetry

I find myself on a quiet hill,
My muse tumbles forth from the quill.
Words so sentimental spill,
flow forth against my will.
Some come like the tide at sea,
The emotions writ beckon me.
Some come hard like the pouring rain,
Like tears that fall with grieving pain.
My heart swells and over flows,
Like the budding of a rose.
Opening to the bright sun,
A different prose each one.
Filling empty spaces,
Satisfying deep dark places.

By Lisa Hiatt

Curling Smoke

Curling smoke from a metallic scented gun,
Still tasted her essence on my tingling tongue.
Thick scarlet blood, like her lips, Laboriously ooze,
Reeking of pungent Channel and cheap booze.
Prone she laid like a cadaver on steel,
Guilt threatening to reject my meal.
Bloodstained sheets our once passion bed,
Void now of love where we once placed our head.
Even in death her lovely body enticed,
My obsession of her was just too high priced.
Sirens are whining rapidly closing in,
Reaching out once more to touch cyanosis skin.
Closing vacant baby blue eyes,
In death the beauty can't tell lies.
Passionately kissing sweet scarlet lips, once more.
Calmly answering the pounds, on the door.

By Lisa Hiatt

Writer's Block

Caught between nightmares and dreams,
In a world where nothing is as it seems.
Riding on dragons with fly paper wings,
Of fairies, trolls and fanciful things.
Wishful thinking leaking from my brain,
Written on paper permanently inked stain.
Tears of gold following down,
To grow yellow roses in the ground.
Verses competing to get out of my head,
With a pen that cries with each word said.
Don't try to understand me,
Stories unfold easy to see.
Sometimes words get clogged if you will,
Writer's block is a bitter pill.
Just keep writing til the medicine works,
And eventually it gets rid of the quirks.

By Lisa Hiatt

Pussy-willows

Fuzzy wuzzy kitten weeps,
Kicking his leg as he sleeps.
Running in slumber-land,
Little tracks in the giant cat-box sand.
Smelly puppy shaped clumps give chase,
In this nightmarish race.
Under the willow tree,
In the shade cool as can be.
Vines from the tree,
Tickling his paw gently.
Warm milk on his whisker drips,
Onto quivering lips.
Tropical summer air billows,
Ironically his name is pussy-willows.

By Lisa Hiatt

Crumbling Dreams

Crumbling dreams made of basalt stone,
All but memories of kingdoms throne.
Tombstones dot fields from battles fought,
From dreams of glory with spoils sought.
Celtic winds lamenting earth bound souls,
Moaning the plight of dooms day tolls.
Tattered colored flags wave behind,
As ghostly warrior forms aligned.
Forever after fighting a war,
From distant lands across foreign shore.
Fairy-tales, dragons, and warrior knight,
For honor, glory and the thrill of the fight.
History books don't write the story,
Of times past in search of glory.
But fabled knights with shiny armor steel,
Echoes of battles beyond surreal.
Romantic notions of times past,
Where dreams are lived but never last.

By Lisa Hiatt

Seashells by the Seashore

Little beach cherubs, shovels in hand,
Mining for seashells in the sand.
Tourists come buy a peek,
Listen to the ocean speak.
Thunder captured with a spell,
Magic found within the shell.
Close your eyes see the beach,
All this within your reach.
Little beach cherubs have found,
Secrets to this wondrous sound.
Let your fertile imagination soar,
Selling seashells by the seashore.

By Lisa Hiatt

Miles

Poppies cluster in open field,
Glorious eyes revealed.
Scarlet faced smiles,
Upturned for miles.
Lay me down in splendor,
Plant my coffin tender.
While vivid-eyed poppies dance,
In glorious field expanse.
Awakening to the sunrise,
Opening brilliant eyes.
The brilliant poppies to my delight,
A haven of rest from my weary plight.

By Lisa Hiatt

Galaxy

Ebony curtain embraces night,
In its wake the stars glowing light.
Fireflies sparkling around the moon,
watching the waltzing Jupiter and Neptune.
Venus and Mars holding hands,
across time, space and distant lands
Pluto and the moon align,
Ushering in springtime.
Constellations within the stars,
From galaxy's canvas afar.
Planets dancing around fiery sun,
Mystical enchantment since times begun.
Holder of the heavens surreal,
Awakener of the seventh seal.
Etched in Stonehenge rock,
Deeply so, that it n'er be forgot.
Bespelling mortals with epic scenes,
From distant pasts and radiant dreams.

By Lisa Hiatt

Candlelight

The solitary house on cemetery hill,
Candlelight on the window-stand gives a chill.
The shutters fallen with disrepair,
Settling house moans a creaking despair,
Sinister shadows gather in the dark of night,
Dancing in the eerie glow of the candle light.
This house on cemetery hill,
Dark and foreboding the air so still.
The creepy house that summons, "Come if you dare."
You can't help but stop to stare.
Tombstones dot the grassy knoll,
Softly the house creaks to the dead to console.
If you watch with a careful eye,
You will think that vision is a lie.
For you'll see an emaciated hand,
Snuff out the candle on the window-stand.

By Lisa Hiatt

Glass

We are forms of intricate glass,
Shaped by our lives and the past.
Some lives irretrievably shattered,
Taken from them all that mattered.
Like flaws in the fragile glass seams,
From heartache and unfulfilled dreams.
We have a choice to live our life,
To either hurt others or embrace our strife.
Choosing to be sharp shards of glass,
Or gentle and kind our choices vast.
Our hearts may be broken a time or two,
But the ultimate choice is up to you.

By Lisa Hiatt

Kendra

My daughter, a letter to you,
Because what's in my heart is very true.
I find myself writing my feelings in poem,
Because I'm hoping it finally hits home.
I see your bright smile in all you do,
I know this is the best part of you.
When I see you I see the child I bore,
I see you have so much to fight for.
Cancer took a part it's true,
But don't let it be the total sum of you
Though you only have one hand,
I do know that God has a plan.
I see your strength where I have none,
I see it in all you've done.
I see the ambition that shines in your eyes,
The same ones that holds out for the ultimate prize.
The heart that never gives in,
When other say you'll never win.
The one who stands up, who'll fight,
The one who tells me it will be all right.
When against all odds you live,
With wholeheartedness you give.
With one hand you'll conquer it all,
Never being one to fear the fall.

By Lisa Hiatt

Diabetes

Words on a page just aren't enough,
Is life supposed to be this tough?
Silence is golden nearly screams to be heard,
When health issues become a nasty word.
Fingers poised over keyboard tense,
Kind words are just a hollow pretense.
Hiding behind masks made of stone,
Having to face the hard feelings alone.
Struggling through life living for tomorrow,
Praying and hoping it has less sorrow.
When words want to come out of the brain,
But are marred from all the heartache and pain.
Pokes from a needle, will they tell,
If diabetes will send you to hell??
Will the doctors have the answers you seek?
Have I been branded weak?
A life of diet and exercise a forced fix,
While the sugars in my blood do nasty tricks
Please don't tell me I'll be okay,
I'm the one who has to live this way.

By Lisa Hiatt

Leprechaun

Beware seacht déag of March my bonne lass,
'Tis a sorrowful sight to see an empty ale glass.
A wee sip for parched lips, and I'll be tellin' my tale,
Of fairies in forest dark and dangerous meadowed dale.
Beware of four leaf clover's luck and leprechaun charms,
Rest assured, you'll be secure here in my arms.
This feisty fey with pot of gold,
promises riches untold.
Beware my bonne gal of Irish charms,
The leprechaun's smile disarms.
He'll whisk you away,
and forever you'll stay.
N'er to be set free,
His woe-some bride you'll be.
If godawful truth be told,
You'll unavoidably grow old.
He's immortal, my bonne sweet,
Brimmin' with fey deceit.
Take heed my bonne gal,
I've done spun my yarnin' tale.

By Lisa Hiatt

Father

Father, I mourn not for your demise,
Your deceit or hurtful lies.
I mourn the father I never knew,

I envy the child with caring dad,
In the swing pushing the lass or lad.
That just was never you.

Father I mourn not for your abuse,
Your childhood was just an excuse.
I don't mind confessing.

I envy the father I never had,
The one I'd be proud to call dad.
Your death was a blessing.

By Lisa Hiatt

Tropicana

Moonlit waves caresses the shore,
Stars shine through heaven's floor.
Tropical winds tease the lush flora,
Scenting the night's ebony aurora.

Harvest moon reflection full,
Waves lapping to the pull.
Drumming within the heart,
Watching the fireflies dart.

The smell of salty waters rise,
Like the moon in solitary eyes.
Tropicana drink in hand,
Warming toes in the sand.

Crickets serenade a romantic tune,
To go with the harvest moon.
Good morning sunny delight,
Stars twinkle good-night.

By Lisa Hiatt

Proclamation

Celestial canvas abundant clouds,
Gray concealing azure shroud.
Springtime flora yawns,
Stretching to new season's dawn.

Heaven's tears falling down,
To awaken the icy hard ground.
Green shaggy carpet on bumpy knoll,
A groundhog peeks from his hole.

Shnuffling the rainy fresh air,
No shadow in the meadow square.
Twitching his nose rather queer,
Proclaiming spring is here.

By Lisa Hiatt

Barren

Mine heart taps but a mortal beat,
Faint from love trodden feet.
Hold gently this tender bird,
Spare thine cruel barbed word.
Softly kiss what's bruised,
Mine heart sorely abused.
Love but a weapon used for pain,
Deeply impaled leaving its stain.
Don't make promises thou can't keep,
Mine condemned heart doth weep.
No lessons learned foolish heart,
Speared again with love's cruel dart.
A time must come to give up trying,
Mine jester's fragile heart dying.
Spare this foolish plight this living hell,
This obscurity I know so well.
Saying good-bye, I bleed no more,
I wage this martyrdom war.
I harden mine heart, as I leave thee,
But even barren it doth not free me.

By Lisa Hiatt

Crimson

Fickle rose a thorn prick soft thine heart,
Blood ebbing from the damage part.
I softly kiss the Crimson tears,
Obscurity mars past yester-years.
Comes valiant care-giver with love's cure,
Laundering the stain again pure.
Unwinding barbed thorn tightly wrapped,
Healing again the heart intact.
Hold close not the prickly thorn,
Cast away doubt and scorn.
Gentling the torrent crimson cascade,
Shaming the perpetrator for damage made.
Love so like thou, crimson rose,
Kindness yet penned in floral prose.
I cradle thine tender heart,
Loving thee in spite of the damaged part.

By Lisa Hiatt

Dear Friend

Hold fast dear friend the burden it seems,
Has murdered all your dreams.
She stole from you your heart of gold,
Leaving your love barren and cold.
I can only comfort you with a tender word,
But I know the endeavor goes unheard.
Forgiveness must come to ease the pain,
For the heart to live again.
It's okay to mourn and grieve,
To keep your heart, pinned to a sleeve.
The tears wash away the stain,
A reminder that loving her was not in vain.
Find solitary comfort in this,
Love comes softly in another's kiss.

By Lisa Hiatt

Worthy

Self-loathing invades the heart,
Hurling the cruel verbal dart.
You're ugly, you're fat, you're not good enough,
You're too short, you're too skinny, you're not so tough.
So many negative vibes,
So much loneliness inside.
As it is, the world is cruel,
Why call yourself a hopeless fool?
You can't even love yourself!
How can you expect others to see your wealth?
When you can look inside,
And see your own-self pride.
That's when others will see,
You *are* truly worthy.

By Lisa Hiatt

Ascend

The creak of the step to ascend,
To destination's end
The drafty room at the top of the stair,
The loneliness that resides there.
The frigid winds that creep to the bone,
A reminder you are born alone.
Bare bulb circles like a flickering firefly,
As time passed by.
Another year has come and gone,
And yet existence on and on.
A soft bed beckons apprehensions descend,
The hollow bitter wind howls extend.
Greedily seeking the warmth residing within,
Maddening ticking clock, silence, dropping of a pin.
The call too strong the urge to rest,
Burdened with sins un-confessed.
Lashes flutter closed, shallow breath,
Surrendering to life's unavoidable death.

By Lisa Hiatt

Descent

The musty room at the bottom of the stair,
Shivers at the creepy crawlies there.
Spiders, beetles, silver fish,
An entomologist's fondest wish.
A specter with phobia intact,
Wishing for existence back.
A second time to do it all again,
Only regrets found at journey's end.
The creaks loud at the descent,
Life selfishly spent,
Too late to repent.
The dirt floor opens wide,
Showing more stairs inside.
Stifling the scream,
At the oily stream.
Creepy crawlies pour,
From the crack on the floor.
Welcome wagon's wishing well,
For the descent to hell.

By Lisa Hiatt

Wicked One

Rapid breath, panting heat,
The heart races a tempoed beat.
Skin feels too tight to wear,
He begins to render and tear.
The full moon shines brightly in his eyes,
He stares into the moon, hypnotized.
Shimmering sweat on sprouting furry skin,
Evil convulsing, impatient within.
He, no longer man but a horror in between,
Amber pupils glowing in the full moon's sheen.
Lethally, the claw rips,
Through once fleshy fingertips.
The pain obvious from the beastly howls,
Blood runs cold with the popping jowls.
Fangs grow and stretch,
The blood races with painful wretch.
Humanity lost when the transformation done,
He is known as the wicked one.

By Lisa Hiatt

Cobwebs and Dust

Open up and peer inside,
It offers a creak as it creeps wide.
Oh joy spring cleaning is plain to see,
Looking around even the cobwebs are dusty.
At least twice a day it seems I must,
Clean away the webby dust.
So through my mind I muck about,
Figuring what is best to throw out.
Opening the windows of my soul,
With a heavy sigh, making a dent my goal.
Feathery quill in hand, I resume,
I sweep the words that have clogged my mind's room.
I vacuum the cobwebs that have clogged me there,
And send out the pages that I can share.
Dust sometimes permeates my mind,
Like writers block leaving its grime behind.
Opening my senses to the fresh air,
Sending out a silent prayer.
Hoping the words come out crystal clear,
For my next poems grand premier.

By Lisa Hiatt

If I Were A Lad

If I were a lad all bold and bright,
I'd cure all ails and hunger's plight.
I'd run a mile and not rest,
And thank the lord and feel blessed.
I'd travel the world to exotic lands,
And walk barefoot in the golden sands.
I'd calm the oceans and clean the sea,
Set the slaves from other land's free.
I'd build love where 'er I go,
And share with other's all I know.
Most of all I'd remain what I already see,
The girl in the mirror just happens to be me.

By Lisa Hiatt

Gossamer

Upon gossamer wings the angels sighed,
Cradling me through tears cried.
Thou downy feathers softly rent,
Comforting the sorrow spent.
Beauty through pain the heart shutters,
The beat but faint it slowly sputters.
Existing with the wrenching pain.
Mine soul sallied with obscure sin,
But thou found the beauty within.
Through hallowed bright halo I see,
Though I be broken thou still love me.
Taking flight to heaven mine soul soars,
Sweet angel of mercy I am yours.

By Lisa Hiatt

Love's First Blush

Compare thou so to blushing rose,
So obscure, I thee pose.
Thine cheeks all abloom with loves first blush,
The heart aflutter with arush.
Butterflies play merrily within,
Secreted thoughts of carnal sin.
A hand quivers with such passion,
In uninhibited fashion.
Moistened lips for throat gone dry,
Wishing so for a distant lover's sigh.
Eyes of emerald glass gaze in wonder,
Mine heart but sunder.
Embrace mine love gentle, sweet sentinel,
Lest I bid thee farewell.

By Lisa Hiatt

My Kingdom

In my kingdom lies a fragile glass throne,
Forbidden is the hurling of stone.
For it may be unseemly seen,
To shatter my glass dream.
My world to me is mine alone,
You may not throw stone.
Cause what is precious to me,
May not be right for thee.
Selfish thoughts? I don't care,
You aren't invited there.
It be my world alone,
My rule repels all stone.
I sit and ponder what may be,
The truth inside sets me free.
I ask not your love or foolish flare,
You aren't invited here.

By Lisa Hiatt

Midnight

Midnight's canvas full with surprise,
Stars twinkle in the skies.
The moon shines in all its glory,

Fireflies dance in the breeze,
Maracas gently rattle from trees.
Crickets chirp the story.

Luna-blossoms smile with delight,
In the glowing moonlight.
Warm waves lap the shore,

Mermaids sing sweetly to entice,
Sailors pay the price.
Smiling serenely descending to sea floor.

Vampires roll their eyes and politely applaud,
Proper etiquette, not wanting to be a fraud.
Politeness is always a must,

Werewolves howl keeping rhythm with the night,
Worshiping the glowing moonlight.
Eyeing the vampires with mistrust.

Gnomes and trolls slither out,
Wondering what the ruckus is about.
Chasing fairies with netting permits,

Fairies giggle with delight,
Dusting the melodious night.
Leaving all with sneezing fits.

By Lisa Hiatt

Love Is

The word is meaningless without attractions,
Love isn't anything without actions.
Love isn't simply a word,
In the dark someone whispered.
It's felt when something's amiss,
In an ardent lovers kiss.
When you gaze into your newborn's eyes,
Something instantly you'll recognize.
An unselfish thing,
Not caring the heartaches it may bring.
Accepting another for even their faults,
Forgiveness from unthinking insults.
For stubborn pride,
At their absence, an emptiness inside.
Love is when you'd die for them,
Love is when you'd cry with them.
Love is grander then, the scheme of things,
Love is the music, your heart sings.

By Lisa Hiatt

Anew

Obscure gloom conceals the sky,
Tempered tears sentimental cry.
Veiled heavens once azure blue,
Laundering winter's obscurity anew.
Spring glorified with gloomy tear,
Vibrant multicolored atmosphere.
Arcing over melancholy gloom,
Revived variegated flora abloom.
Butterflies harvest the bounty of spring,
While enjoying the music robins bring.
Lazily flutter-by dancing one on one,
Basking under the hidden sun.
Bedazzling the pouty gloom,
Intoxicated by flora's heady perfume.

By Lisa Hiatt

Mine Love

I cometh hence on bended knee,
To ask forgiveness of thee.
Mine heart hath remained true,
Though circumstances hath gone askew.
Prison bars n'er thee hold,
Nor keep me from thine threshold.
Take heart mine love though life obscured,
I hold thou within mine heart secured.
With tenfold of warrior knight,
To rescue thee from thine prison plight.
I take thee from thy errand strife,
To make thee mine future wife.
Hold fast in true n'er prison can bind,
Though circumstances unkind
For without thou by mine side,
Mine heart hath hence forth died.

By Lisa Hiatt

Knight

O bliss be found,
My heart love bound.
My blackened soul once sold,

My chivalrous knight waged,
Hell's demons engaged.
Breaking Satan's hold.

Ardent kisses awaken dormant passion,
Turning obscurity ashen.
Gentled the beast's thunder,

Clasp softly my heart's trepidation,
Thou art mine salvation.
Mine chains that bind but sunder.

By Lisa Hiatt

Daisy Head

Melancholy willow in dreamland deep,
By the icy river counting sheep.
Awaiting spring's awakening,
The sounds of ice breaking.
Rosebuds eager to burst,
Warm rains quench the thirst.
The rainbow leaks its color down,
To flowers in the dormant ground.
Crocus impatiently peeks,
Stretching towards the warmth it seeks.
Upturned yellow faces,
Aligned in furrowed spaces.
Tulips merrily shine,
With colors divine.
Dissipate the lingering snow,
Variegated hues aglow.
Flowers tell the willow "Get out of bed,
Spring is here daisy head."

By Lisa Hiatt

Gypsy

She danced with grace and charm,
In sultry seduction with raised arm.
Around the flames that hotly burns,
With fancy swirls and intricate turns.
Poetry in motion around the fire,
A gypsy tune softly played from a golden lyre.
She tells a tale of sadness she'd mourn,
Her heart heavy and forlorn.
Ebony eyes shine with a tear,
For her lover's, no longer here.
He left her on this mortal plane,
While he went to heaven to reign.
The wave's gentle tambourine kept tempo as she stepped,
Salt misty water mingles with tears she wept.
The music swells with the ember's heat,
Long midnight hair swayed to the beat.
So like the embers spark, her lover's eyes burned,
Oh how her heart mourned and yearned.
Night creatures watched entranced,
Hypnotized by the rhythm she danced
A rainbowed skirt like bellows fanned the fires,
Her brow glistened with perspires.
The full moon aglow on the sea's wrath,
Her bare feet in the silky sand marked a path.
All through that summer's eve till dawn kissed the dark,
Exhausted she dreamt of his ember eyes that spark.

By Lisa Hiatt

www.ingramcontent.com/pod-product-compliance
Lightning Source LLC
Chambersburg PA
CBHW042056290426
44111CB00001B/23